Cornish Time

Marc Harris

First published 2025
by Rowanvale Books Ltd
The Gate
Keppoch Street
Roath
Cardiff
CF24 3JW
www.rowanvalebooks.com

A CIP catalogue record for this book is available from the British Library.
ISBN: 978-1-83584-055-9
Hardback ISBN: 978-1-83584-056-6
eBook ISBN: 978-1-83584-057-3

Cornish Time

Marc Harris

DISCLAIMER

I would like to stress that all information provided in this book was accurate at the time of publication.

CONTENTS

INTRODUCTION

In 2012 I completed a wonderful and special cycling and walking odyssey across southern Cornwall. I cycled and walked from Penzance to Liskeard, with much of the cycling and walking being around the precipitous coast.

My journey encompassed many fantastic locations, where I met fascinating people, encountered stunning wildlife, and sampled some of the delicious local produce the county of Cornwall has to offer.

I stayed in some memorable locations, such as the Housel Bay Hotel on the Lizard Peninsula, where rugged cliffs are battered by onshore winds and waves, and secret, tiny coves are littered with golden sands.

My journey took me to such beautiful places as Cadgwith Cove, the Lost Gardens of Heligan, and the lovely town of Fowey, as well as many more isolated locations where the sea was turquoise and the sun lit up the cliffs.

Apart from the personal account of my journey, which took place in 2012, I have included in this book updated information about various places and attractions which I either encountered in that year or intend to visit in future.

The Eden Project, the Cornish Seal Sanctuary, and the charming, historic port of Charlestown are covered in detail in the pages of this book, and are places I will visit in years to come.

My journey in 2012 was something of a pilgrimage for me, as I was recovering from an exceedingly painful series of knee operations, and the rugged coastline of Cornwall provided me with just the challenge I needed to complete my recovery.

I hope you enjoy this book, and I hope it encourages you to visit some of the superlative locations and discover some of the wonderful wildlife I encountered in 2012.

My cycling and walking odyssey was life-affirming and will remain with me for the rest of my days.

It remains, to this day, one of the best experiences of my life. Enjoy.

ACKNOWLEDGEMENTS

I would like to thank the following organisations that gave me invaluable inspiration and help with this book:

The Cornish Seal Sanctuary, the Eden Project, and Visit Cornwall.

I also could not have completed my book without the genuine warmth and hospitality provided by the wonderful people I met in Cornwall in 2012.

So, a big thank you to them.

CORNISH TIME

A WALKING AND CYCLING ODYSSEY

I was told the locals called it 'Cornish time'. I guess it was a sense of not knowing what day it was, or even what time it was, and how the passage of time in such stunning surroundings really had little meaning.

I was on a journey, approaching my fiftieth birthday, and about to spend seven days walking and cycling around the southern coast of Cornwall. I would cycle one hundred and thirty miles in all and walk another twenty. I would cycle up and down many hills, get lost a few times, and be blown from my bike into a ditch as a huge articulated lorry roared past me on a quiet country road, sweeping me into a tangle of nettles and brambles. But with only injured pride and a few sharp pricks and stings to contend with, I would soon recover. And a few days into my journey, as I relaxed in the beautiful village of Gorran Haven, four miles south of the Lost Gardens of Heligan, I would experience what it really meant to become one with 'Cornish time'.

I arrived in Penzance, by train, at the beginning of August 2012. I had left my home city of Cardiff some five hours earlier, locking my mountain bike in the carriage close to my seat. After studying my map closely, I made the decision to cycle towards the Lizard Peninsula, where I hoped to find accommodation for the night. It was great to be on my bike again and in the open air after the somewhat claustrophobic confines of the train.

The cycling was easy as I left Penzance. I passed St Michael's Mount whilst following the coastal path for a few miles before the terrain became more difficult as I approached the town of Helston. I had been forewarned about the very hilly nature of southern Cornwall – a fact that became increasingly apparent as my journey progressed! So, it was quite refreshing to come across one of the few flat areas of my trip while on the A3083, which bisects the Royal Naval Base at Culdrose.

By the time I arrived in the village of Lizard in the early evening, some four hours and twenty-seven miles after leaving Penzance, I was rather hot and quite tired. I was looking for somewhere to stay for the night, and eventually found the Housel Bay Hotel. The hotel is the most southerly located hotel in Britain and a fine example of late Victorian architecture, built in the early 1880s with the approval of the then prime minister, William Gladstone. The Cornish Coastal Path runs through the hotel gardens and provides access to some of the most magnificent locations on the British mainland. With a near perfect position on Lizard Point, the Housel Bay Hotel overlooks the western approaches of the Atlantic Ocean, where it meets the English Channel. Guests can relax watching the endless procession of ships leaving the Channel, or enjoying glimpses of sandy Housel Bay Cove, nestling just beneath the cliff at the front of the hotel.

I could not quite believe just how beautiful my location was. After some much-needed food and a couple of pints of Cornish

Rattler – a cider made at the St Austell Brewery – I fell blissfully asleep in my room.

Sometime during the night, I was awoken by what I assumed to be thunder and lightning. The rain was hammering against my window as the wind lashed the storm against the glass. I sat up in bed, rubbing my bleary eyes, before peering outside into the darkness. I was amazed to see that the flashes of light came not from any bolts of lightning, but from the twin towers of the Lizard Lighthouse, perhaps half a mile from the hotel. For some time, I was transfixed. A lighthouse flashing eerie signals through my bedroom window in the middle of the night – what more could a man want from a holiday in such stunning surroundings! Eventually, I drifted wearily back into a dream-filled sleep. Ghostly galleons, the benign spirits of drowned sailors, and long-dead smugglers were to dominate those dreams.

I awoke early the next day, showered, then made my way downstairs. The previous night's storm had abated and now it was a wonderfully sunny August morning. I sat in the breakfast lounge of the hotel, enjoying my cooked meal of locally sourced produce and absorbing the heat of the summer sun, which had already warmed the interior of the building. The view from the lounge was magnificent. Beyond the hotel gardens, the waters of Housel Bay Cove shimmered with a turquoise iridescence, whilst the golden sands of the beach would not have seemed out of place on any tropical island.

After breakfast, and on the advice of the hotel proprietor, I decided to walk the Southwest Coastal Path to Kynance Cove, a round trip of about eight miles. It is not possible to cycle this section of the coastal path, and indeed, cycling is banned for most of its length, as apart from the often precarious footpaths, much of the path has populations of rare plants and animals, and these unique habitats could be destroyed by the actions of cyclists. In fact, the hotel and adjoining gardens are part of a Special Area of Conservation, and that day, I was really hoping to see one of the iconic animals which so typified the wildness of this area of Cornwall, a magnificent black bird with a bright red beak: the chough. A member of the crow family, the birds had recolonised the rocky coastline in tiny numbers, possibly from Europe, and were now nesting and breeding amongst the cliffs. I set off from the hotel just after nine o'clock that morning with a camera, a good pair of binoculars, and a rucksack containing the day's essentials.

My walk to Kynance Cove varied in degrees of difficulty. At times I was quite close to the cliff edge, but there were many flat sections of the coastal path, well away from any precipitous drops. And indeed, the flatter sections of the path could be accessed by both young and old alike. I walked for about four hours, passing Lizard Point and the lighthouse which had flashed those eerie signals into my bedroom the previous night. The lighthouse is now a heritage centre. I also encountered the 'most southerly house in the British Isles', the now defunct lifeboat station, a cafe, and a gift shop. The gift shop sold various ornaments fashioned from serpentine rock, the rock from which much of the coastal landscape is constructed.

In places where the path fell sharply away to the sea, it was very narrow, winding up those rugged cliffs like a snake. On the flatter sections of the path, further away from the cliff edge, I chatted to some of the walkers I met. A couple sitting on a bench who must have been well into their eighties told me, as they stared out to sea, 'We will remember this view for the rest of our lives.'

I could hardly have disagreed, and as I peered down from the clifftop and into the sea, I spotted the whiskery faces of a pair of grey seals, their inquisitive heads bobbing up and down in the swell like wine corks. A kestrel hovered above me, perhaps only fifty feet from where I stood, using the strong onshore winds to help it hover as it hunted for prey in the grass below.

As the summer sun beat down from the cloudless sky, I was optimistic that it would not be long before I saw a chough. The next bird I saw, however, was a pied flycatcher, a small black and white bird, which darted between the grass stems in search of insects. I also encountered other creatures, including a millipede crawling along the footpath, and one of the largest species of British butterfly, a member of the fritillary family. It was difficult to tell if the butterfly was a dark green fritillary or a silver-washed fritillary, but it was obvious from the sheer size and brilliant colours of the insect that it was one of these majestic giants. It was a special sighting for me.

It was soon after this that I saw my target species: the chough. It was great to see one in Britain, and it was wonderful to see that these black crows with distinctive, downturned beaks had returned to this stretch of the Cornish coastline. I did not even need my binoculars to view the bird as it perched on a windswept clifftop some one hundred feet from where I stood. Although with the aid of those binoculars, the view of the bird and its bright red beak was even more spectacular. For what seemed an age, it remained on the cliff edge before flying off into the distance and disappearing over the sea. The sighting of the chough had made my day; anything else I saw now would just be a bonus.

Soon after, I arrived at Kynance Cove. There were already many people on the beach, including several surfers. This spot, with its cafe and swathe of golden sands, was extremely attractive and family friendly; but to some extent, I had come to Cornwall to get away from people, so I decided not to stay long. I began my return journey to the hotel, satisfied with what I had seen that day. The views had been stunning, the wildlife wonderful.

That night, after some food and a couple of pints of Cornish Rattler, I drifted into a deep sleep. Outside, the lights from the Lizard Lighthouse permeated the blackness of the still Cornish night.

I awoke early the next morning. The weather was fine and the skies azure blue. It was not a difficult decision to spend a second day on the Lizard Peninsula and a second night in the Housel Bay Hotel. After another delicious cooked breakfast, I thought I might take a leisurely walk into the village of Lizard itself. The previous day, on my clifftop walk to Kynance Cove, one of the locals had told me about the possible location of some adders. He had seen a nest of them close to a five-bar gate on one of the footpaths which leads inland from the clifftops to the village. He had also told me that one of the female adders was pregnant, and that it was the biggest and fattest adder he had ever seen! Sadly, despite my best efforts, I could not locate the gate, nor the adders.

The village of Lizard is very pleasant, with a village green and quaint shops which cater for tourists, but not in the tacky, tasteless way that some places do. One of the local treats, which I would recommend anyone trying, is Roskilly's ice cream, which comes in all manner of unusual flavours. I had a daily craving for this ice cream and downed many cornets throughout my journey across Cornwall, in the main because I was often hot and dehydrated from either cycling or walking, and the cornets had the much-desired effect of cooling me down. Although I must say,

I've never really needed an excuse to eat ice cream. Roskilly's was one of the best ice creams I had ever tasted, and it was a pleasure to experiment with the different flavours! After eating a pasty – of course I had to try one – I took a leisurely stroll back to the hotel, along the coastal path.

I had decided to take it a little easier that day, so I thought I would cycle to the traditional fishing port of Cadgwith, a relatively short distance of some eight miles from the hotel. The descent into Cadgwith is quite steep, but the village itself is absolutely stunning, with picture-postcard views. As I sat on the harbour wall, staring down into the translucent, shallow sea, I became transfixed by the small shoals of fish which glinted like jewels in the golden sunlight. A few traditional fishing boats were moored on the stony beach. Cottages and houses, some with thatched roofs, and magnificent flower-filled gardens give Cadgwith that chocolate-box image of quaintness that I for one was more than happy to embrace. It was not difficult to imagine those traditional fishing boats tilting and riding on the 'fishingboat-bobbing sea' as the tide came in, just like the line from that famous Dylan Thomas play, *Under Milk Wood*.

Later, after wandering the leafy lanes, exploring some of the shops and an art gallery which promoted the work of local artists, I cycled back up the hill and returned to the hotel.

That evening I sat in the hotel gardens, enjoying some sandwiches while watching the sun go down and the light fade across the sea. As my mind drifted with the clouds, I sensed that I could have stayed in the area for another week, such was the beauty and magnificence of the Lizard's wonderful coastline, but for my journey's sake, I knew that I had to move on. I would check out the next day and head for Falmouth.

I vacated the hotel the following morning; I had a real feeling of sadness to be leaving such a beautiful area behind. Without doubt, staying at the Housel Bay Hotel was a wonderful experience, and I would recommend it to anyone. I knew that I would return to stay at the hotel in the years to come, to spend more time walking and exploring the magnificent Lizard coastline.

I was heading for the Helford River, where I would put my bike on the ferry, and cross the river in the direction of Falmouth. My journey was pleasant, with clear, sunny blue skies. I arrived at Helford Passage in the early afternoon, having crossed the sparse heathland of Goonhilly Downs – a site made famous by the huge satellite dishes of the Earth Station, which are visible for miles. The Downs are part of a Site of Special Scientific Interest, where adders and stonechats are common. The raised plateau on which the Downs sit was also one of the few flat areas I had cycled across since leaving Penzance. I can say, without equivocation, that this flat, straight road was a welcome relief for both mind and body alike!

The heathland is also home to many rare plants, including the Cornish Heath, which has been adopted as the county flower.

A welcome light shower accompanied me as I left the sparse landscape of the Downs behind. Some three hours later, I was making the steep and snake-like descent into Helford Passage; the brakes on my mountain bike were tested to their limit.

As I crossed a small ford, which spanned the river at one of its narrowest points, one of the locals ushered me in the direction of a jetty from which the ferry departed. I had no idea what time the ferry left, and I was a bit dismayed to arrive at the jetty just at the point when the boat (which was little more than a small river cruiser) was leaving for the opposite riverbank! I had missed the crossing by minutes and would now have to wait for three hours for the tide to turn and the ferry to come back.

On the upside, I now had plenty of time to explore my surroundings. Having locked my bike to some railings, I wandered up and down the riverbank, turning over stones and exploring the myriad rock pools in the hope of discovering some rare marine creature, with all the enthusiasm of a seven-year-old child. As in most years gone by, all I really found were a few prawns, a crab or two, and the odd dead mussel. Still, it was great to feel like a child again, even if I had not found the remains of a giant squid, or some yet to be discovered prehistoric monster!

After indulging in some inquisitive rock pooling, I headed to a local pub, where I ate locally caught crab and seasonal salad sandwiches. After that wonderful lunch, I cycled back to the jetty to await the ferry's return. As I lay on the slipway, using my rucksack for a pillow, the August sun lulled me into a light, dreamy sleep.

Sometime later, I awoke to the sight of the small ferry chugging its way across the estuary. As the boat pulled up alongside the jetty, the helmswoman explained to me that it was fine to put my bike on her small craft. In only a matter of minutes I was on the other side of the Helford River and cycling up a steep hill in the direction of Falmouth.

It had taken me three hours to cycle the twenty-eight miles from the Housel Bay Hotel to what seemed a veritable metropolis! My journey from the most southerly point in the British Isles, the Lizard, had taken me up and down many hills, so after cycling around Falmouth for a while, and really feeling quite fatigued, I booked myself into a rather basic B&B. I calculated that at this point, since getting off the train in Penzance, I had cycled a total of sixty-four miles and walked more than ten in the vicinity of the Lizard Peninsula. I was grateful for a rest, hot coffee, and a shower, and although the B&B was nothing like the luxurious Housel Bay Hotel, it was clean and tidy, and that was all that really mattered.

After a brief nap in my room, I took a leisurely stroll into the centre of Falmouth. I explored the waterfront, admiring the myriad ships of all shapes and sizes, including several small warships anchored in the harbour. I sat on the quayside, where I enjoyed a Chinese takeaway.

It was early evening before I returned to my B&B. It was only when I switched on the television in my room that I realised I had not used any technology for three days and had almost forgotten that the London Olympics were taking place. But to me, that act of not switching on the television was really what 'Cornish time' was all about. I was losing myself in other, more valuable pursuits.

I fell asleep on my bed, just after Usain Bolt streaked to victory in the one hundred metres. It turned out to be a genuinely great spectacle, and despite my break from technology, I must admit that I was secretly quite glad that I had witnessed such a momentous event.

The following day, I woke early and made my way to the quayside in Falmouth, where I booked myself and my bike on to the ferry for the crossing across the Fal River to the picturesque village of St Mawes. There is only one road out of St Mawes which, of course, is up a very steep hill! The weather remained good, with clear blue skies interspersed with occasional cotton-wool cumulus clouds.

Although a light breeze accompanied me on my journey, I soon worked up a sweat as I followed the A3078 a mile or two inland from the coast in a north-easterly direction towards Very-an Green. This was marked on my map as another picturesque village. I then joined National Cycle Route 3, after cycling some ten miles from St Mawes. My journey was quite arduous at times, with the constant cycling up and down hills taking its toll. I was longing for some continuous straight, flat road which stretched for some distance over the horizon. But I concluded that, with me being so close to the coast, and this being Cornwall, this scenario was about as likely as me winning the Tour de France!

I still had no idea where I would end up that day, and in total I would cycle twenty-six miles before I found my accommodation for the night. Again, the views I encountered from all the coves were stunning, which more than compensated for the fatigue that was now creeping into my legs. I was often hypnotised by the tranquil, turquoise-blue waters which lapped against the golden sands of many of these secret little bays. And, to top it all, as I got off my bike for a rest and to take in another of these wonderful views, I was to glimpse the form of a particularly rare, and rather plump, lizard scuttling across the road in front of me. The view of this lizard became another important sighting for me as, hav-ing seen many smaller common lizards before, I was positive that I had just encountered a beautiful and scarce male sand lizard. This was another first for me, and although my sighting had been fleeting, I was thrilled to have seen one of Britain's most colourful and exquisite reptiles!

Four hours after leaving Falmouth, I found myself cycling down the steep descent into the stunning coastal village of Gor-ran Haven. Up to this point in my journey, I had cycled ninety miles and walked a further ten along the rugged paths of the Liz-ard Peninsula. Despite drinking plenty of water, I was quite dehydrated and ready for a rest as I booked myself into a picturesque B&B in my eventful trek across southern Cornwall.

Once I had replenished myself with copious amounts of fluids, the owners of the small B&B told me a tale of a German couple who had stayed with them in a previous year while cycling south towards Land's End. How far the couple had cycled to get to Gorran Haven, the proprietor of the hotel could not remember, but what he did say was that the couple had become quite ill, having clearly underestimated the difficulties of the steep, undulating landscape of this part of England. He said that the couple had no choice but to stay at the B&B for two days, until they rehydrated themselves and recovered their strength and resolve to continue their journey. I could certainly understand why.

That night, I wandered in the direction of the beach, and to the only chip shop in the village – a chip shop that was so busy with locals and holidaymakers alike that it always ran out of fish by eight o'clock and was forced to close at that time every night. And I could see why; I would have to say that those were some of the best fish and chips I had ever tasted.

After enjoying my meal whilst sitting on the quayside and watching the sun set over the sea, I took a short, leisurely walk to the top of the cliffs, overlooking the bay. As I sat quietly on a bench, absorbing the sounds and scents of the gathering dusk, a mixed flock of swallows, house martins, and swifts trawled the sky for insects only feet above my head. Below me the small sandy cove had emptied of human life, and my thoughts turned to a poem I had written about swallows some years before. It is a favourite poem of mine, and one which encapsulated the scene above me in a nutshell.

SWALLOWS

Like darting fish
flashing in the shallows
they trawl the slack,
swallows.

They come in waves
with fins for wings
to fish the ocean sky,
trawl the slack –
suck their minnows dry.

'Cornish time' had swallowed me up, and I was so grateful that it had. Time, and the days of the week, had become an irrelevance, and that made me happy and content. I was in a tranquil place as I approached my fiftieth birthday.

The next day, I woke to the sounds of cows lowing somewhere in the distance of the mist-shrouded morning, and nesting herring gulls which scratched and scuttled about the roof above me. Today I would cycle four miles south to the Lost Gardens of Heligan.

The gardens were magnificent! And when the sun appeared from behind the clouds it made my visit to Heligan even more breathtaking. It was a place I would recommend to anyone, with ample parking space and a visitor centre which caters for all age groups. There were hides overlooking ponds where you could observe all manner of aquatic and non-aquatic animal life; they also included many interactive tools which would appeal to children and adults alike. There were herb gardens and a wonderful variety of trees and shrubs from all corners of the world, including specialist growing areas where rare plants from countries such as New Zealand flourished in the temperate climate.

It was wonderful to discover large ponds where beautiful, red-finned roach and rudd swam in huge shoals, surrounded on the banks by great ferns and lush, luxuriant water-loving plants. In the shimmering heat, the roach and rudd seemed to hover just below the water's surface, like an armada of miniature submarines; they were completely at peace and in tune with the serenity of their world.

I was exceedingly reluctant to leave the ponds as they had a soothing, hypnotic effect on me and let my imagination run away with itself. But I knew I had to move on, so after walking through the depression known as the Lost Valley, I wound my way back towards the visitor centre to enjoy an ice cream and a brief meander around the shop. Half an hour later I was cycling northwards towards St Austell.

My initial thoughts on arriving in St Austell were that I would stay in a B&B and visit the Eden Project, but in the end I decided to cycle onwards in the direction of Fowey, a place that had been recommended to me by the owner of the last guesthouse in which I had stayed.

As usual, there were many undulating hills on my cycle to Fowey. By the time I arrived, some twenty-two miles after leaving Gorran Haven, I was feeling fatigued, and once again, despite my best efforts, I was quite dehydrated. The cumulative effect of almost a week's hard cycling and walking was beginning to take its toll on me.

As I descended the steep gradient into Fowey, I came across a very attractive-looking B&B, with numerous flower-filled hanging baskets adorning the building's walls. The owner of the premises informed me he had a room for one night, perhaps two. I asked him if he had anywhere safe I could lock my bike. I will remember what he said to me for an exceptionally long time!

'Oh, you don't need to lock your bike! No one is going to nick a bike in Fowey! They might nick a boat, but not a bike!'

My reply, in my somewhat rather exhausted, dehydrated state, went something along these lines: 'No one is bloody likely to nick a bike anywhere along the bloody southern coast of Cornwall! There are too many damn hills!'

He was a large, rather rotund man, not dissimilar to the bearded actor Brian Blessed, and his raucous, bellowing laughter merely seemed to confirm my assertion that he thought I was a little mad for cycling all the miles that I had.

I pushed my bike into an old outhouse for safekeeping (where it remained unlocked) and retired to my room. After a short rest, I decided that I would be staying in Fowey for two nights. I knew that tomorrow there would be no cycling for me. My mind and body were telling me that I needed a good rest, and that is just the way it was to be.

That night, after a pub meal and a brief look around the shops and harbour, I lay on my bed to watch more of the Olympics on the television. I am proud to say that I witnessed Mo Farah scorch to victory in the five thousand metres. London and the Olympics seemed a million miles away, but once again I was glad that I was able to witness more from such a remarkable event.

Although the decision to stay two nights in Fowey was really made for me by the levels of fatigue I felt, Fowey was such a lovely, picturesque port that I was grateful to be able to spend some time exploring the town on foot.

The next morning, I headed off towards the centre of town. It was great to amble through the streets, leafing through the second-hand bookshops and wandering the art galleries full of work by local artists. After a while, I came across an old, rather dilapidated building close to the quayside, which I was incredibly pleased to see housed the Fowey Aquarium. I decided to visit, and it was very enjoyable to observe the range of marine life, both large and small, patrolling their tanks. This marine life included both lobsters and pollack; some of the pollack were close to ten pounds in weight.

I felt like a kid in a sweet shop again! I was taken to a world of wave-swept rock pools where mini-beasts, including crabs, gobies, and blennies, darted between translucent prawns and shrimps, which frolicked in their environment as if they were in the open ocean.

Chatting to the owner of the aquarium, it was wonderful to hear that once the fish had grown too big for their tanks, local fisherman would return them to the sea, where they might grow into real giants. The fish would then be replaced by freshly caught smaller members of the same species. This was to be the case with the ten-pound pollack, which were about to be returned to the ocean from whence they came. It was great to see that the people cared about the creatures in their charge, and that the animals were not just there as moneymaking exhibits.

After reluctantly leaving the aquarium, I wandered the side streets of Fowey. As I walked along the main street, I was amazed to see a man motoring gingerly towards me in an electric wheel-chair, accompanied by what I could only assume were his elderly parents and a pair of parrots! Yes, parrots! Each exquisitely feathered bird was tethered loosely to his shoulders. At first, I thought

I was seeing things. But having spoken to the man, I learnt of his affection for his birds. He could not bear to leave them at home, so he had brought them on holiday with him and was now simply taking them for a walk!

This made me think of my two rescue cats, Chi-Chi and I-Ching, which I had left incarcerated in a cattery near Cardiff. It was their first time in a cattery, and they had been extremely nervous, and seeing the parrots made me realise just how much I was missing them. I knew then that it was time to return to Cardiff.

That night, I wandered the quayside of Fowey, enjoying a pint, some great food, and some people-watching. Later, to the background noise of more triumphs at the London Olympics, I drifted off to sleep.

In the morning, I checked out from the B&B and crossed the Fowey Estuary by ferry to the picturesque village of Polruan, before climbing the hill in a north-easterly direction towards Liskeard, where I would catch the train back to Cardiff.

It rained steadily for the whole of the sixteen-mile journey to Liskeard station. This, perhaps rather fortuitously, was the only day of my seven-day trip when it had rained. So, considering the dreadfully wet summer we had in 2012, I counted myself incredibly lucky that I had encountered such great weather. Despite my waterproofs, I was soaked to the skin.

As I sank into my seat on the train, I felt tired, yet in some ways truly invigorated.

In my relaxed state of mind, I reflected on my journey. I had really enjoyed my cycling odyssey across southern Cornwall. I had cycled one hundred and thirty miles in all and walked a further twenty miles along the coastal path, much of it around the Lizard Peninsula. I had eaten some wonderful food, stayed in some beautiful locations, and seen some magnificent wildlife. Yes, the cycling had at times been hard, and I must have burnt off thousands of calories, but I knew that one day I would return to Cornwall and continue my cycling and walking pilgrimage around the stunning county.

Four hours later I would be back in Cardiff. I thought fondly of my two cats and, although I had felt very guilty about putting them in the cattery, I hoped they would be really pleased to see me. As I drifted off into a light sleep, I knew that I would remember my cycling and walking holiday across southern Cornwall for the rest of my life.

POSTSCRIPT

My cycling odyssey across southern Cornwall was really something of a pilgrimage for me. I have always enjoyed cycling and have cycled thousands of miles over the years. Being on two wheels gives you the freedom of the open roads and allows you access to the natural world in a way that is in part lost to those who use motorised transport. I must stress that I am not against cars in any way. To some, cars are a necessity, to others, a luxury of vanity. But you sense more of nature when you are cycling or walking, and sometimes nature comes to you, when clearly this would not be the case should you be driving. My cycling journey across southern Cornwall brought me remarkably close to nature.

In some ways, my journey was cathartic. Between 2009 and 2011, I had four operations on my left knee, was unable to work, and was registered disabled for two years. I was on crutches for much of this time, had some serious orthopaedic surgery, and was in chronic pain throughout. I never had the best posture as a child, having broken a bone in my right hip in my early teens, which later led to an operation in my early twenties. My posture, I believe, had in some way contributed to the overall deterioration and condition of my knee. Although in some ways, as the surgeon said, I was just unlucky, with one condition developing after another as my knee deteriorated.

On the brighter side, the nurses who treated me said I was bionic! And, of course, as medical professionals, I had to agree with them wholeheartedly! Eventually, I made a full recovery, went back to work, and began to cycle again. So, it was just wonderful for me to visit southern Cornwall and complete my solo cycle ride. I was well again, and that was all that really mattered.

Perhaps, subconsciously, I had a second reason for cycling across Cornwall. A great uncle of mine, William Best Harris, now deceased, had been city librarian in Plymouth from 1947 until 1974. He wrote several books about Devon and Cornwall, many of which are still available to this day. Uncle Bill spent nearly eight years walking most of the coastline of Devon and Cornwall with his wife Betty, researching details for a weekly broadcast for the BBC radio programme *Morning Sou'West*. Honey, their golden Labrador, walked with them – starting the long trek as a puppy and ending it as a middle-aged lady! William Best Harris died in 1987, at the age of seventy-three.

CADGWITH

Cadgwith is a small fishing village, almost forgotten by the 21st century. It can be accessed on foot from Lizard Point if you follow the Southwest Coastal Path in a north-easterly direction, and the route passes near several landmarks including the Lizard Lighthouse, the coastguard lookout, the Devil's Frying Pan (a collapsed sea cave) and historic wireless and signalling stations. A full guided walk is available through the iWalk Cornwall app for Apple or Android phones. But if you are a bit old-fashioned like me and you think you might get lost, a good Ordnance Survey map may be just the thing you need!

The village itself is stunning, with picture-postcard views. A stream winds its way down the valley, trickling over the sand and shingle beach, and white-washed cottages with thatched roofs scattered on either slope seem to typify everything an idyllic Cornish village should be. Cadgwith is a place to relax, enjoy the stunning scenery, and simply absorb the atmosphere in such wonderful surroundings.

Cadgwith today is still a real working village. Fishing boats leave the beach daily, weather permitting. Nowadays the catch is quite different from in the past. Pilchards, which were once caught in their millions and were previously the mainstay of the Cornish fishing industry, have now been replaced by catches of crab, lobster, mackerel, shark, and mullet. Yes, the catch has changed, but a way of life that has existed for centuries still proliferates. The village remains the focus of social life, and folk music and Cornish singing are ever-present.

Everywhere, there are reminders of past generations. There is the old lifeboat house, which was still in use until 1963, old pilchard cellars, and memories of those in the fishing community who lost their lives to the sea. These things are carefully preserved, and without doubt treasured, forming part and parcel of the tight-knit fabric of the village itself.

From spring to summer, the moors, cliffs, and hedgerows are alive with birdsong and adorned with wildflowers. And tranquil, balmy summer days in Cadgwith Cove can surely only enhance a bygone simplicity that was once so typical of many Cornish coastal villages.

If you wish to stay in Cadgwith itself, there is self-catering and bed and breakfast accommodation available, and the Cadgwith Cove Inn faces the sea, caters for families, and has a 4-star rating. But if you wish to stay nearby, on the Lizard Peninsula, I would personally recommend the Housel Bay Hotel.

Yes, the village of Cadgwith is a great place to visit; try it for yourself.

THE LOST GARDENS OF HELIGAN

The Cornish translation of 'Heligan' is 'Willows', and the Lost Gardens of Heligan have been the seat of the Tremayne family for over four hundred years. Over the centuries, various generations of the Tremayne dynasty, after the building of Heligan House in 1603, developed the gardens. Between 1766 and 1901, walled flower gardens and shelterbelts were constructed, and rides were designed. The construction of shelterbelts was designed to protect the gardens from the brutal storms which batter the area from the south-west. Links with exotic plant-hunters were established, Home Farm began to thrive, and the acquisition of new and exotic species nurtured the development of the Japanese and Northern Gardens. At the end of the nineteenth century, Heligan was in its prime, but with the outbreak of the First World War the gardens sank into a state of disrepair, strangled by a tangle of vegetation, with years of neglect to follow. The gardens simply disappeared, as if vanishing into the ether.

Perhaps by some miracle, in 1990, after a hurricane in that year, the gardens were rediscovered. A small room in a corner of one of the walled gardens, which had been buried beneath a pile of masonry, was exposed, and in that room an inscription was found pencilled into its walls: 'Don't come here to sleep and slumber.' The inscription was then signed by those who had worked on the gardens just before the outbreak of the Great War; presumably before many of them went to fight in the trenches – a poignant reminder perhaps for some of those who, without doubt, would never return to work in the tranquillity of the gardens of pre-war Cornwall.

The Lost Gardens of Heligan reopened to the public in April 1992, having been restored with the diligence and exceptional hard work of several voluntary organisations such as the BCTV, whose restoration work was severely constrained by the limitations of a tiny budget. The gardens have now become self-funding. Grant aid, which was provided by various organisations and public sources after 1992, has now ceased, and the Lost Gardens of Heligan have become a viable business with the aim of providing full employment, with obvious benefits to the local and wider community. With such a dedicated team, whose aims are to nurture and foster the relationship with the land as it used to be, as it is now, and as it can be in future, this 'sleeping beauty of a landscape' now sustains and provides a haven of some two hundred acres to explore.

Here you will encounter ancient woodlands, a sub-tropical jungle, orchards, pioneering wildlife projects and sustainable farmland. The farm itself has now been awarded 'Rare Breed Farm Park Status', and some of its menagerie of livestock, such as endangered breeds of sheep and cattle, graze on ancient pasture. Bamboo tunnels, giant luxuriant ferns and banana plants flourish. Without a shadow of a doubt, Sleeping Beauty is wide awake, and she is thriving in the form of the Lost Gardens of Heligan.

In the eighteenth and nineteenth centuries, various generations of the Tremayne family continued the development of the gardens. For example: the long drive to Heligan House was planted, the ravine built, and Italian gardens constructed. During the First World War the building became a convalescence hospital for officers, in the Second World War it was occupied by American officers, and in the 1970s the house was converted into flats.

So, we come to 1990, when the inscription in the wall of the Thunderbox room was discovered by Tim Smith and John Willis – the latter being a descendant of the Tremayne dynasty.

In 1990, John Nelson, now deceased, began the clearance work.

Since that time, the gardens have been meticulously restored. Some examples of that restoration include the clearance of the vegetable and sundial gardens, the restoration of the lakes in the Lost Valley, and then the opening of the Lost Valley itself. The New Zealand Garden was replanted, Heligan calves were born, and two TV series – which I watched with utter fascination – were made by Channel 4.

During the twenty-first century, the gardens have received many accolades including being awarded a gold medal at the RHS Hampton Court flower show, and being voted the 'Nation's Favourite Garden' by BBC *Gardeners' World*. Visitors have flocked to Heligan in their thousands, and *Springwatch* have filmed in the gardens' stunning surroundings on more than one occasion.

In spring, Heligan is simply just a delight to behold. The woodlands are a carpet of bluebells, and wildflowers proliferate. After the dark, bleak, brooding days of winter, the gardens become a riot of colour, alive with the sounds of birdsong, and embrace the arch-pollinators – the moths, butterflies, bees, hoverflies, and all manner of insect-life which are so essential to the health and vitality of so many of the plants and trees.

There are greenhouses, herb and flower gardens, and a wonderful variety of trees and shrubs from all corners of the world, including specialist growing areas where rare plants from countries such as New Zealand flourish in the temperate climate.

POSTSCRIPT

Without doubt, The Lost Gardens of Heligan are simply a remarkable place – growing over three hundred varieties of fruits and vegetables, for example, and being the largest garden restoration in Europe. Some quotes about Heligan include: 'The Garden Restoration of the Century' from *The Times*, 'Paradise Discovered' from the *Sunday Express*, and from John Craven in BBC's *Countryfile* magazine, 'A glorious tribute to Britain's gardening heritage.'

What more can I say – I don't think I could have put it any better myself!

You can find the Lost Gardens of Heligan at:
The Lost Gardens of Heligan
Pentewan
St Austell
Cornwall
PL26 6EN
www.heligan.com
Tel: 01726 845100
Email: info@heligan.com

THE CORNISH SEAL SANCTUARY

The Cornish Seal Sanctuary is a wonderful place to visit. The sanctuary is owned and run by the Sea Life Trust, a registered charity.

The centre is located near the village of Gweek, on the banks of the Helford River, where its mission to rescue, care for, and treat grey seals and other marine mammals who have been injured, or suffered harm in any way, is such an admirable one. The aim of the centre is then to release the rescued seals back into their natural environment. If, for any reason, an injured animal cannot be returned to the sea, then they are given a permanent home within the sanctuary.

Seal pups are often separated from their mothers and cannot feed, and this is when the centre's role as rescuers becomes so vital.

The sanctuary's beginnings go back to the late 1950s, where its founder, Ken Jones, found a baby seal washed up on a beach near his home at Saint Agnes. By the mid-1970s the solitary pool at Saint Agnes was too small for the growing population of rescued seals, and a new location was found at Gweek, which has developed into the sanctuary that exists today, where that one pool has now become five.

Education and inspiration are two of the principles the sanctuary holds close to its heart. As such, visitors can attend a seal talk, where they are informed of the unique history of individual animals, including rescued grey seal pups. These pups can be observed in the harbour view pool, interacting with the adults, where they learn about catching fish, an essential requirement for survival if they are to be returned to the open sea.

The seals can be observed from the underwater viewing areas, and are a delight to behold as they frolic and twist and turn in their watery haven.

The specialist seal hospital treats and rehabilitates over seventy grey seal pups annually. These pups have been rescued locally, and once they have achieved a weight that is considered healthy, and their injuries have healed, they can be returned to the wild.

To treat and restore a grey seal pup to health costs approximately £2,000 per annum. Some injured and malnourished seals cost more to treat, simply because of the seriousness of their injuries, which are often caused by entanglement in fishing gear which may have been lost by accident, deliberately discarded, or detached during storms. These entanglements, or 'ghost nets' as they are known, can be a magnet to an inquisitive seal. Ghost nets can float freely in the sea, or lie on the sea floor, and are a pernicious blight on our oceans, along with plastics, which can also cause serious injury or even death to marine mammals as they are ingested or, as in the case of flying rings, which are used by some people for entertainment on beaches, become a noose which tightens around the animal's neck. As the seals grow, these flying rings sink deeper into the animals' flesh, and as stated above, cause horrific injury, which may lead to the agonising death of the unfortunate animal.

A good thing, perhaps, that on some beaches in the UK, flying rings have been banned.

Donations to the centre are most welcome, however small. A donation for such a wonderful cause can be made by card payment or by direct debit. Even a one-off payment of £5 is not inconsequential and will do something to help rehabilitate a seal or marine mammal.

A fundraising project, Fund Our Future, aiming to raise £1.3 million is now in place, seeking to secure the legacy of the sanctuary and build more facilities to enhance the quality of a seal's life while it is under the care of the trust. Proceeds will go towards building a brand-new filtration system, designed to improve water quality and clarity, which will be great for the seals' health and public viewing alike. Other improvements to the sanctuary, generated by any fundraising, will include creating a brand-new covered viewing area which will be seated. Money will also be directed to improving access to pools for the carers, which will improve and enrich the lives of the resident seals and other sea mammals.

With this all in mind, it is hoped that the sanctuary will continue to inspire and educate an ongoing interest in marine mammals, and nurture an interest and fascination for the work conducted at the sanctuary for years to come.

There are many ways in which members of the public or businesses can help the centre. For example, £50 pays for a full vet visit for a rescued pup. Just a small donation of £10 enables the sanctuary to purchase toys which keep the seals entertained and improve the quality of environment in which the mammals find themselves. £500 covers essential surgery which could save a seal's life.

Examples of fundraising activities through which members of the public may raise money for the centre include Gift Aiding your ticket to the sanctuary, taking part in a sponsored fun run, leaving a gift in your will, or simply volunteering for seal rescue work. Business sponsorships are also available, and more information can be found on the sanctuary's website.

Ticket prices range from £20.99 for an adult to £17.99 for a child under sixteen. There are discounts for students and senior citizens, and carers for people with disabilities are allowed in for free. Booking online is the easiest option. Tickets remain valid for a year, so can be used at future dates. Children under sixteen must be accompanied by an adult.

Experiencing what the sanctuary has to offer is, of course, a wonderful experience. Gift vouchers are available so that you can, for example, have breakfast with the seals. Here you will visit the seal hospital and learn the history of rescued seal pups. You will also be able to feed the seals, scattering fish into their enclosures and watching the animals feed. This package includes a lovely continental breakfast and access to the centre for the remainder of the day. Other packages include 'keeper for the day', where you get an opportunity to get close to the seals, learn about preparing fish and cleaning out their enclosures, and find out about seal releases into the open sea.

Beavers are now also resident at the sanctuary and may be viewed in their large woodland enclosure. You will also be able to enjoy seeing the penguins and rescued Icelandic puffins, which are now resident at the centre.

Paddock animals such as rare breeds of sheep and goats are present within the sanctuary.

Packages for school visits are also extremely popular, and children can see for themselves what a fantastic place the centre is.

The centre is also dog friendly, so you can bring along your canine companion. Access is available to most areas within the centre, with only a few exceptions.

The public can support the centre in other ways by sponsoring a pup. If you do so, you will receive a pup adoption pack. Amongst other benefits, you will have the opportunity to name a seal, be allowed one visit to the centre, and have the chance to attend the release of the animal into the open sea. Pup sponsorship is available for the sum of £300.

For those seals which have made the sanctuary their permanent home, because they are not robust enough to be released, adoption packs are available for £45, plus £5 P&P.

Work experience placements and internships are available, where you can work at the centre for specified periods of time, learning everything about the day-to-day care of the seals. You will assist with preparing food, attend vet visits, seal releases, and enhance the animals' lives through training and enrichment.

Yes, the Cornish Seal Sanctuary at Gweek is well worth a visit. The Sea Life Trust and its staff and volunteers do an incredible job rescuing and rehabilitating seals and other marine mammals.

But without the public's help, the sanctuary would struggle to survive. I urge you – do what you can to help the centre continue its magnificent work.

Our oceans, as we now know, are in a perilous position. Saving seals and other animals is just a small part of what we, as a human race, must now do to rescue our planet and the animals who are suffering because of human history, which has done so much damage to our environment.

Please help the sanctuary in any way you can.

Please see the sanctuary's website for further information and updates, particularly regarding ticket prices, entry times, and current events.

You can find the centre at:
The Cornish Seal Sanctuary
Gweek
Cornwall
TR12 6UG
www.sealsanctuary.co.uk
Tel: 01326 221361
Email: seals@sealifetrust.com

THE EDEN PROJECT

The Eden Project is located three miles from St Austell, where it was constructed on the site of an old china clay pit.

The complex that exists today is vastly different from those old clay-pit workings. Nowadays, futuristic domes, known as biomes, house species-rich environments simulating, for example, a rainforest and a Mediterranean ecosystem, which flourish inside the shelter of these protective biomes.

Opened in the year 2001, the Eden Project has become a magnet for visitors who have come in their millions, generating considerable wealth for the Cornish economy.

If you are coming by car, parking is free onsite, and there are electric vehicle charging points within the complex. A bus service stops at the project, and the nearest train station is only a few miles away at St Austell. Part of the on-road National Cycle Network, Route 3 runs adjacent to the Eden Project, and of course, walkers are actively encouraged. The project has also been designed to aid those with a disability to access all areas.

Those wishing to visit the project are advised to pre-book tickets during the busiest times, such as school holidays. At other times, tickets are available on arrival. Those who have become passholders, either as an annual or as a local passholder, will need to pre-book a timed entry slot. Becoming a member of the Eden Project costs, at present, £56.50 per annum, and gives you discount in the shop, restaurants, and cafes, as well as discounts on courses and certain activities. You will have delivery of the *Eden* magazine, which brings you all the latest news about the project, and unlimited free entry to the site, with options for bringing guests.

Members of the public are also offered a guided tour experience, where, for example, the deeply knowledgeable guides will take you on a tour of the rainforest and Mediterranean biomes. Other tours will take you on a journey where you can immerse yourself in Eden's history, learn about the spice gardens and the lush, luxuriant plants which populate the rainforest complex. For times, prices, and booking details it is best to check out the project's website.

Visits for schools are actively encouraged, and the education team offer curriculum-centred learning suitable for children of all ages. Looking at the 'What's On' feature on the website is strongly advised.

Gardens typical of those found in all corners of the world are on display. Plants proliferate with perfumed scents and vibrant colours in gardens such as the Western Australia Garden and the South Africa Garden. In the microcosms of the Amazon rainforest, South-East Asia, West Africa, and tropical islands, moisture-loving foliage dominates the biome. A canopy walkway gives stunning views of the scene below.

The vital importance of the arch-pollinators, such as bees, butterflies, and moths, come to the fore in the 'Plants for Pollinators' exhibit, reminding visitors, if they are not already aware, that so much of the world's food production is implicitly reliant on the diverse insect population which inhabits our planet. The project is also the home for the National Wildflower Centre, and wildflower habitats are created across the country using seeds stored in the project's wildflower bank.

Nature's Playground, a wonderful wild and interactive play area for children, is open throughout the year. Entry to this attraction comes with your admission ticket. Children, of course, must be supervised by an adult, particularly as water features are included in this sensory experience, and the children are liable to get wet!

Climate change is on so many people's agendas, as it is now apparent that we are in a climate emergency. Examples of what the project is doing to address this issue include agreeing to become a climate-positive organisation by 2030, thereby attempting to remove greenhouse gases from the atmosphere, creating carbon sinks and protecting the natural environment. The project is also committed to constructing future Eden Projects in other locations around the United Kingdom and abroad. These will generate their own reusable energy, will be low carbon, and will recycle resources. Much of the food used at Eden is sourced locally in Cornwall, and food waste is used onsite to feed the plants after being recycled in an aerobic composter.

Education, is, of course, one of the defining principles of the project. A plethora of learning opportunities are provided for all ages, from pre-school children to adults at colleges and universities. Programmes are designed for teachers, and degree courses are provided through learning at the project, with degrees in plant science just one of the courses on offer. Online courses are also covered, and the RHS Level 2 Certificate in Plant Growth and Management can be a way to help the individual pursue a career in horticulture, or simply stimulate an interest in botanical skills for personal development.

In the case of children, more than 50,000 children a year are welcomed to the project for workshops and school visits. Eden can be 'the best classroom in the world', according to Tim Smit, the project's co-founder.

Future Eden Projects are planned for Dundee, Morecambe in Lancashire, China, Costa Rica, and other locations across the world.

As a charity, the project's mission is to create links that bring people and nature closer together, facilitating an environmental movement that can care for our planet.

Surely, this is something worthwhile accomplishing.

Our planet is in dire peril. We must do everything possible to save it.

Donations to the project can be made by various means, including by pledging a monthly sum, or through JustGiving.

Please check the website for further information including updated ticket prices, entry times, and membership details, etc.

The Eden Project can be found at:
The Eden Project
Bodelva
Cornwall
PL24 2SG
www.edenproject.com
Tel: 01726 811932
Email: info@edenproject.com

CHARLESTOWN

Charlestown, just over a mile from St Austell, was once a historic maritime port.

With stunning views across the harbour, the port, once built to export china clay and copper to South Wales from its grade-two listed harbour, has now become a magnet to visitors who revel in the Georgian character of its buildings, which sit near traditional pastel fisherman's cottages and harbourside inns. Quaint shops nestle amongst delightful eateries, where local food and drink are the mainstay of the tourist industry.

Nowadays, the main industry – apart from tourism – associated with Charlestown is the film industry. The port has often been used as a film set. The series *Poldark* was filmed in Charlestown, as was *The Onedin Line*. The village has, for example, also been used in the production of a version of *Alice in Wonderland*, and the film *The Eagle Has Landed*.

A visit to the Shipwreck Treasure Museum is also a must-see if you visit the port. Here, you can view thousands of artefacts, taken from over 150 shipwrecks, which dot the rugged coastline. You will also have the chance to enter some of the tunnels once used to transport china clay to the ships that once graced the harbour.

In the harbour itself, you may get the chance to see one of the visiting tall ships which make use of the facilities, or even glimpse the Danish tall-ship *Anny*, built just before the Second World War, which makes Charlestown its home. In the future, the plan is to attract and train young people to crew a variety of vessels based in the port.

Staying in Charlestown itself is a magical experience. The Rashleigh Arms, named after Charles Rashleigh, the entrepreneur who developed the port in the late 18th century, has won awards for its hospitality. You can stay in one of its attractive rooms and enjoy local food and drink from the delightful menu, which is sourced from the myriad local produce which the county of Cornwall has to offer. Dog-friendly rooms are available, and dogs are welcomed in the bar.

Quaint cottages are also available to rent within the village and in the surrounding area, and small hotels such as the Pier House Hotel, which overlooks the harbour, are a wonderful place to stay, with great food.

Yes, Charlestown is certainly worth a visit. See it for yourself.

Please contact Visit Cornwall for further information at:
Visit Cornwall
30 Boscawen Street
Truro
Cornwall
TR1 2QQ
www.visitcornwall.com
Tel: 01872 261735
Email: visitcornwall@truro.gov.uk

AUTHOR PROFILE

Marc Harris was born in Cardiff, Wales, the United Kingdom, in 1962.

Marc has previously written four books and a poetry pamphlet.

The natural world has always been a wonder to him, and the themes of nature and the environment always feature strongly in his books.

His previous books include *Wild and Uncanny Tales* – a tribute to the Gothic horror tradition, *South and West Wales: Its Wildlife, People and Places, Wild Tales and Rural Rides*, a poetry book – *Rhythms of Nature*, and the poetry pamphlet *Sentience*.

Marc has also written for magazines such as *The Countryman, Explore England*, and *This England*.

A lover of cycling, he has cycled thousands of miles in his lifetime, often in pursuit of his fascination with nature and wild places.

He now lives with his two rescue cats, in a house in Dinas Powys, in the Vale of Glamorgan. His cats keep him constantly entertained and are wonderful companions which he adores.

WHAT DID YOU THINK OF *CORNISH TIME*?

A big thank you for purchasing this book. It means a lot that you chose this book specifically from such a wide range on offer. I do hope you enjoyed it.

Book reviews are incredibly important for an author. All feedback helps them improve their writing for future projects and for developing this edition. If you are able to spare a few minutes to post a review on Amazon, that would be much appreciated.

PUBLISHER INFORMATION

Rowanvale Books provides publishing services to independent authors, writers and poets all over the globe. We deliver a personal, honest and efficient service that allows authors to see their work published, while remaining in control of the process and retaining their creativity. By making publishing services available to authors in a cost-effective and ethical way, we at Rowanvale Books hope to ensure that the local, national and international community benefits from a steady stream of good quality literature.

For more information about us, our authors or our publications, please get in touch.

www.rowanvalebooks.com
info@rowanvalebooks.com